MY FIRST ARABIC LETTERS
FOR NEURODIVERSE LEARNERS

RIZIA BEGUM

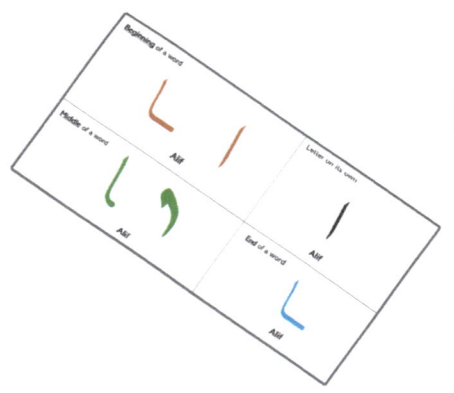

My First Arabic Letters

For neurodiverse learners

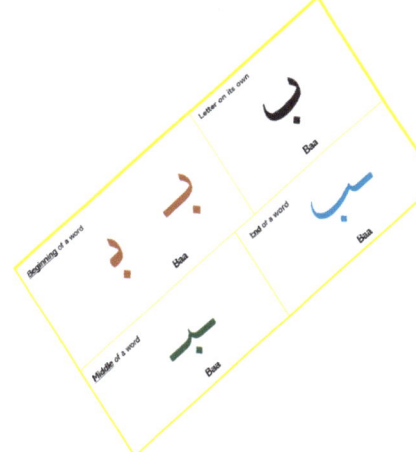

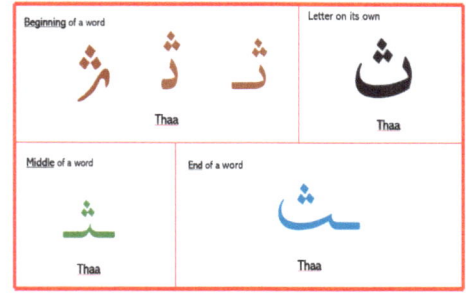

Rizia Begum

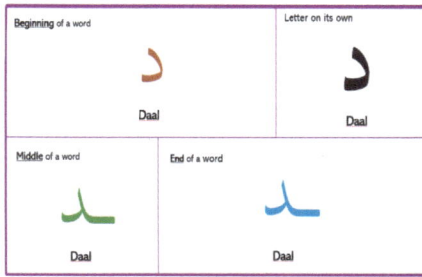

'This book is dedicated to... Sulaiman and all the children like him.'

Biography

Rizia Begum is a PGCE qualified Specialist Teacher in Speech, Language, Communication and Autism / ADHD. She is the CEO and the director of the registered company, Inspired SEND Learning, a training centre that delivers wide range of courses, both online and in person to clients from public, co-operate, governmental and private sectors.

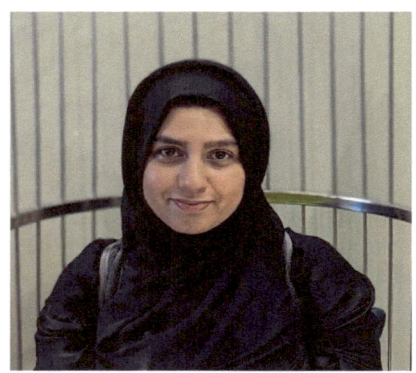

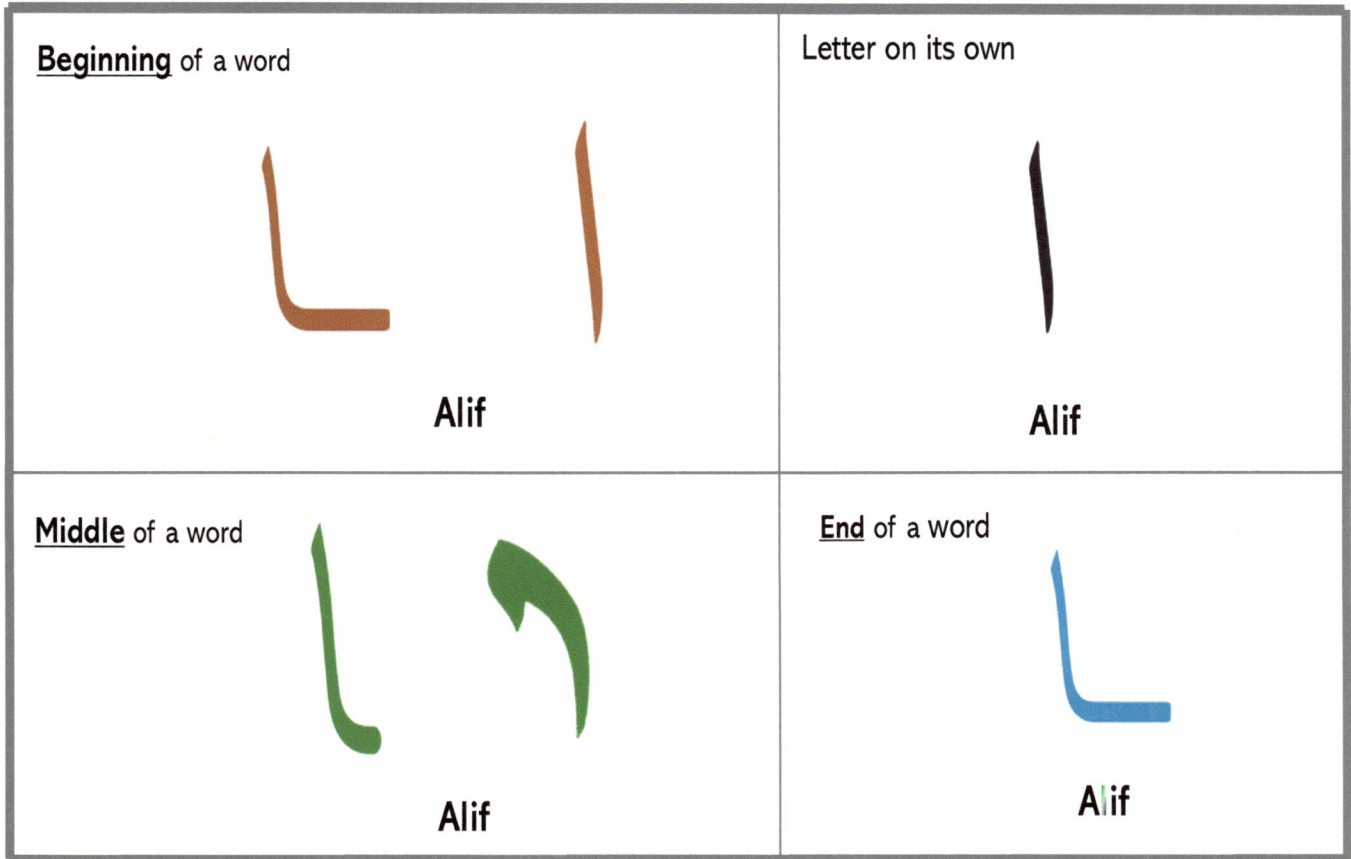

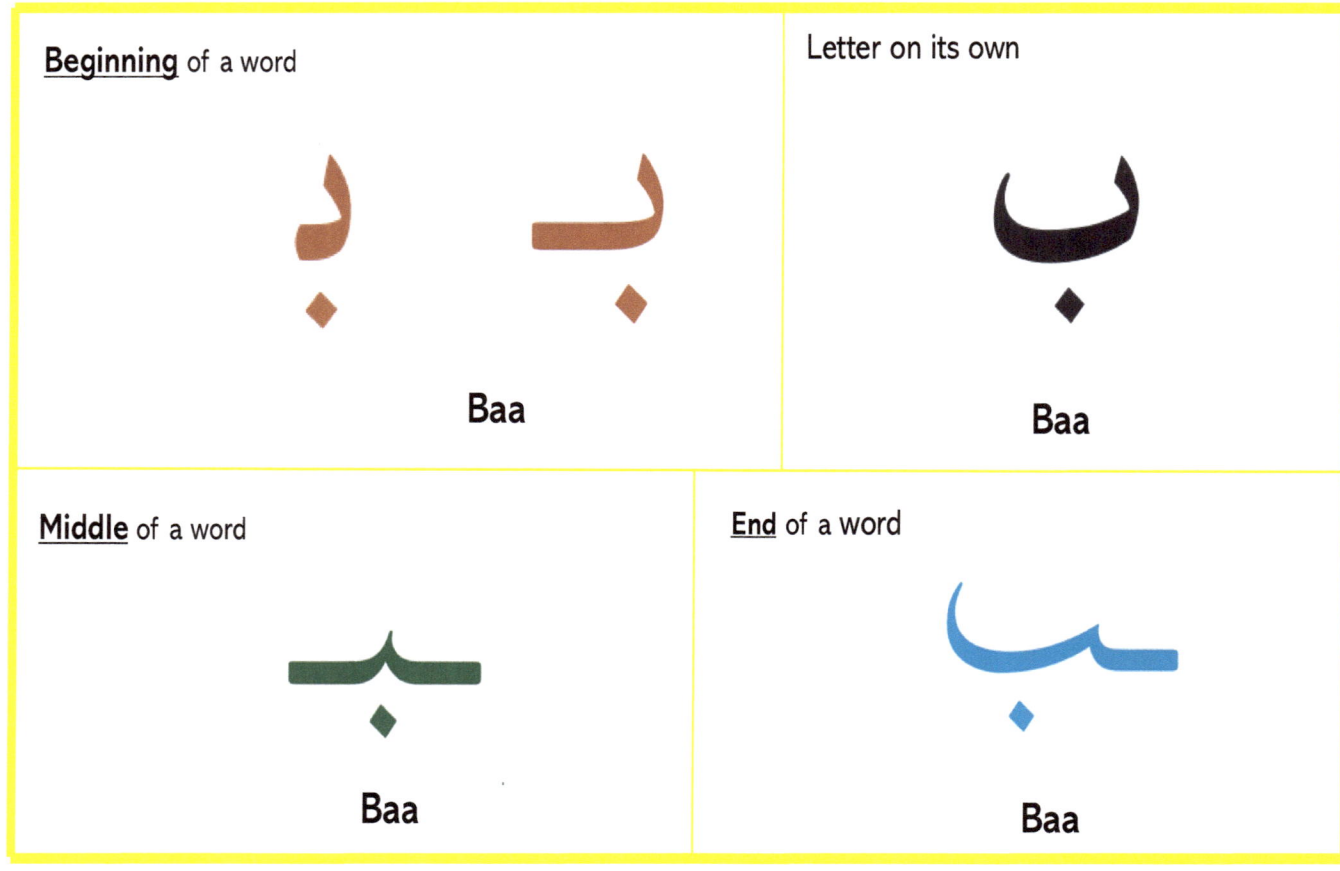

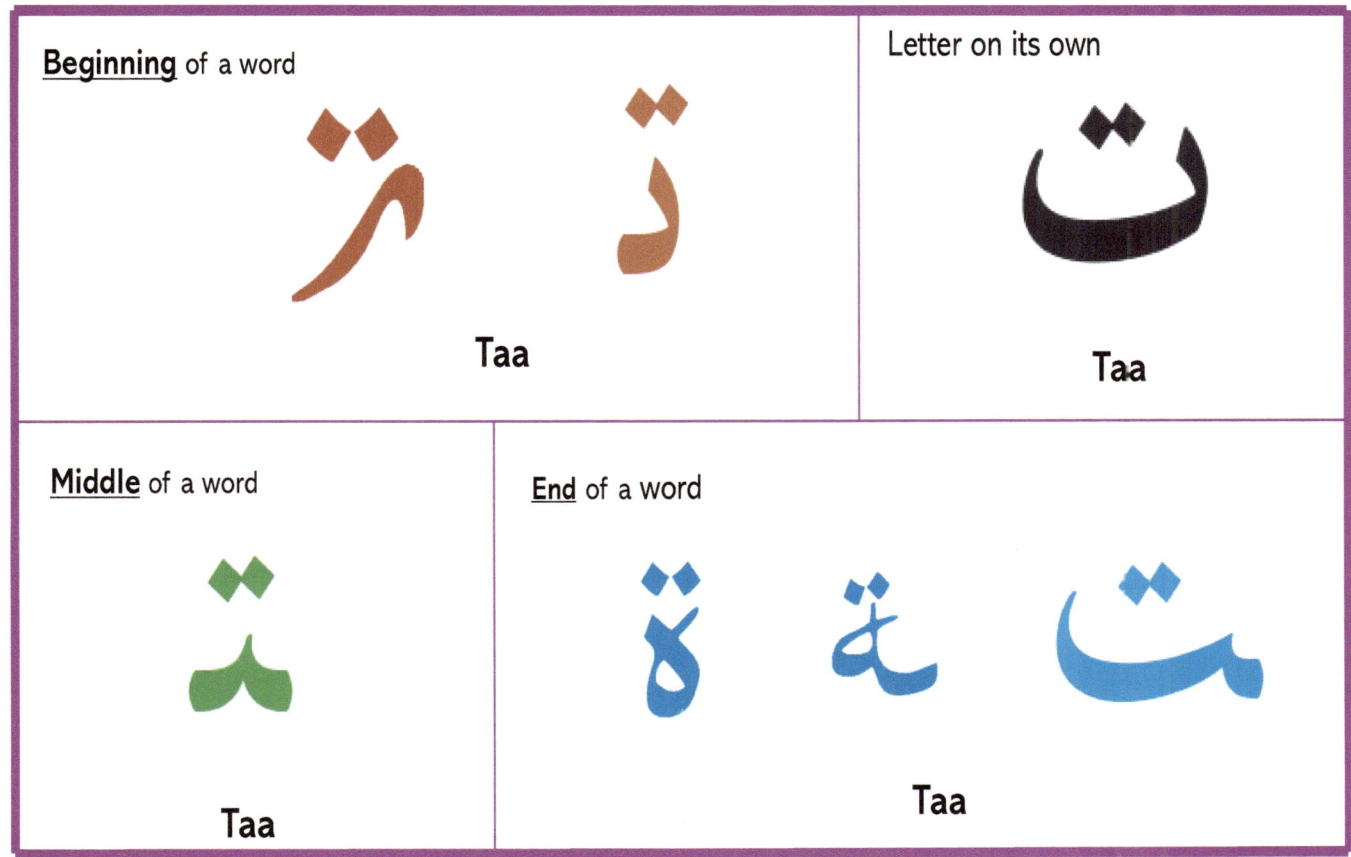

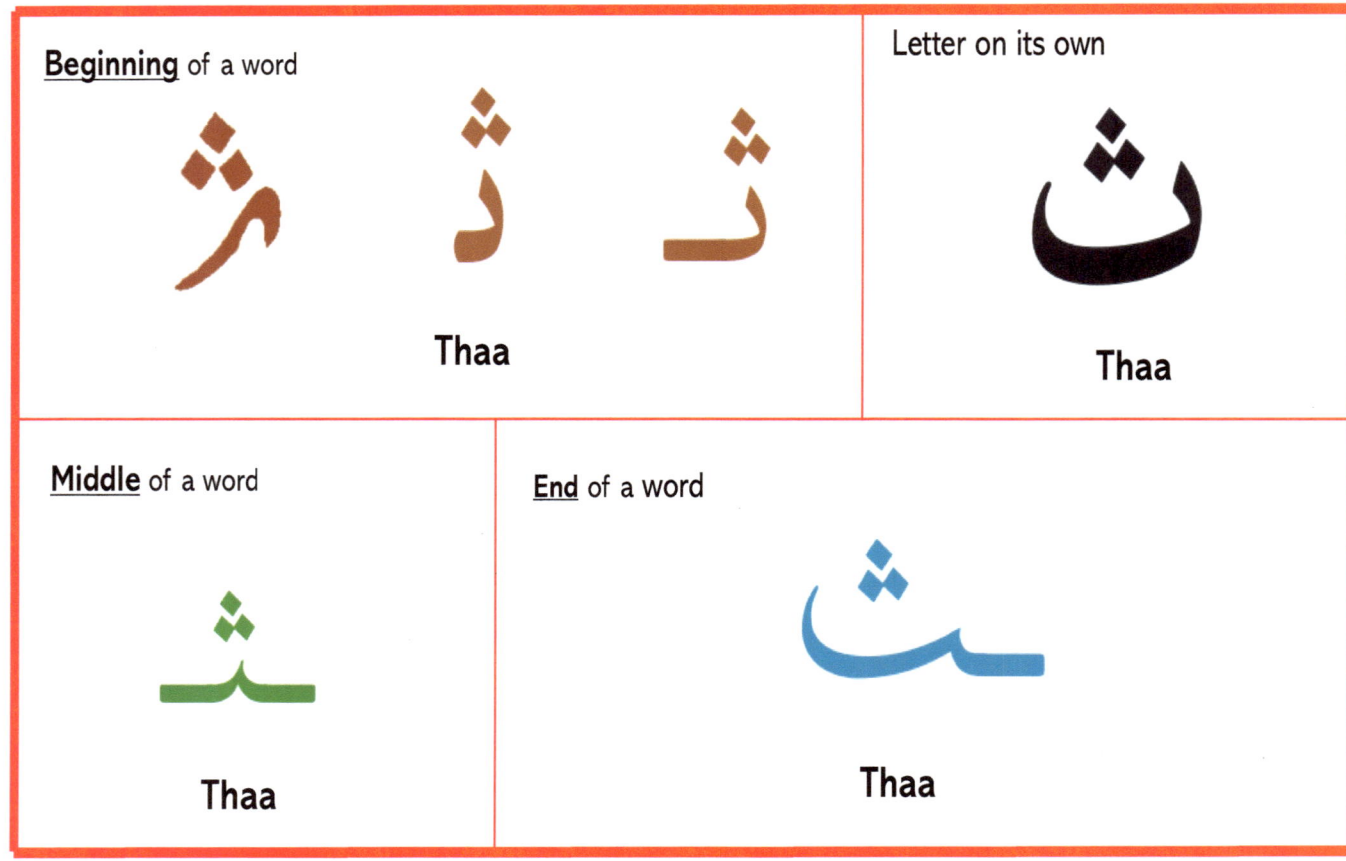

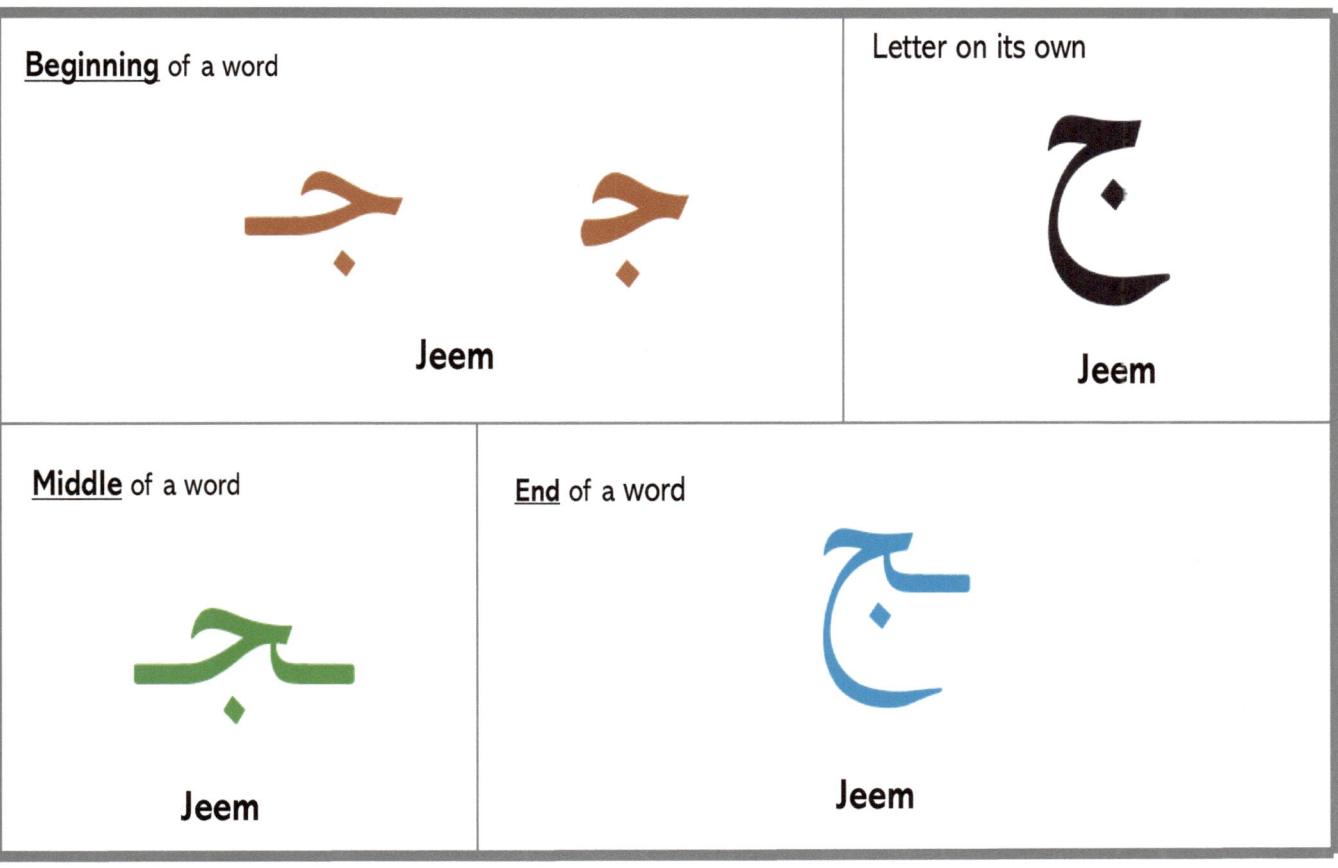

Beginning of a word ح ح Haa	Letter on its own ح Haa
Middle of a word ح Haa	**End** of a word ح Haa

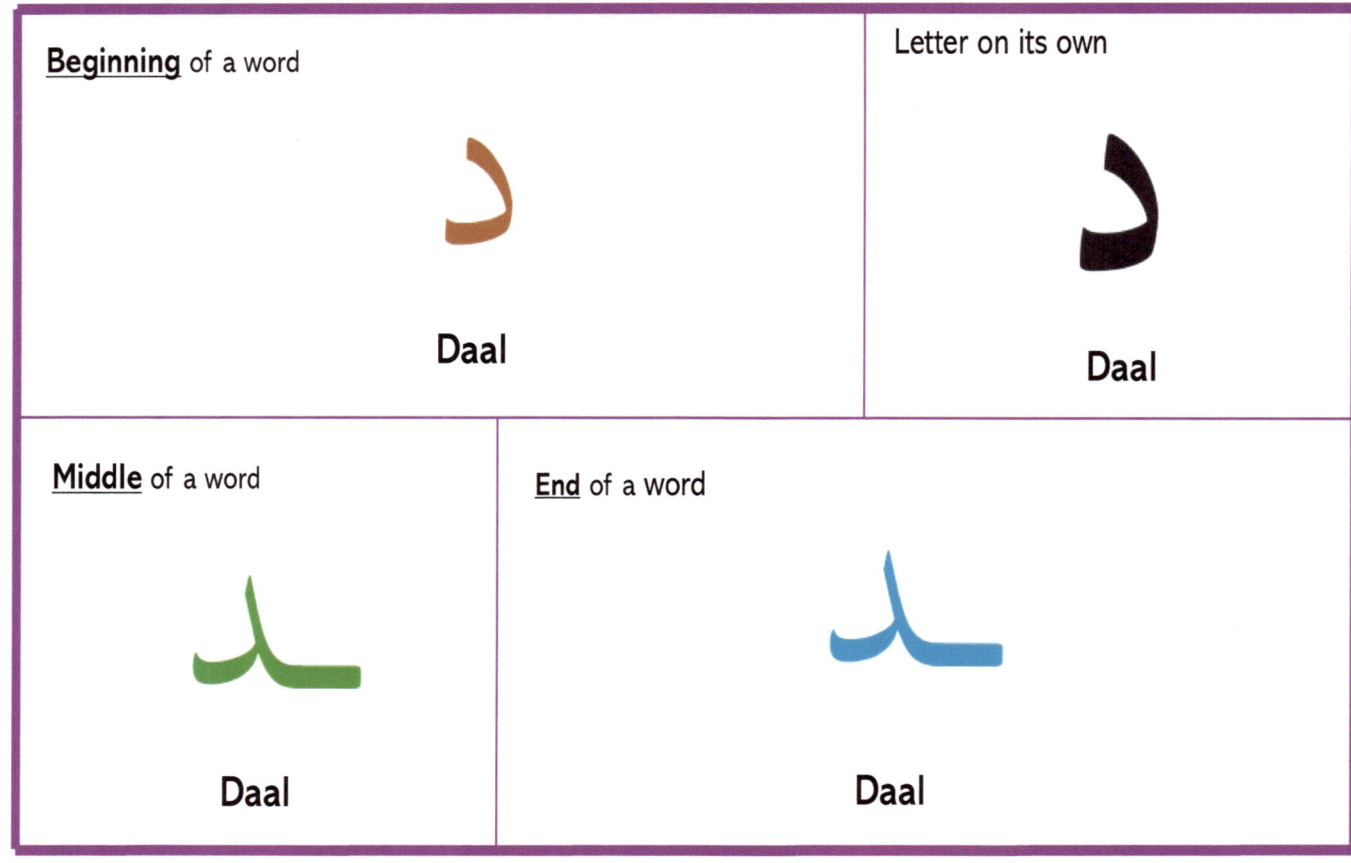

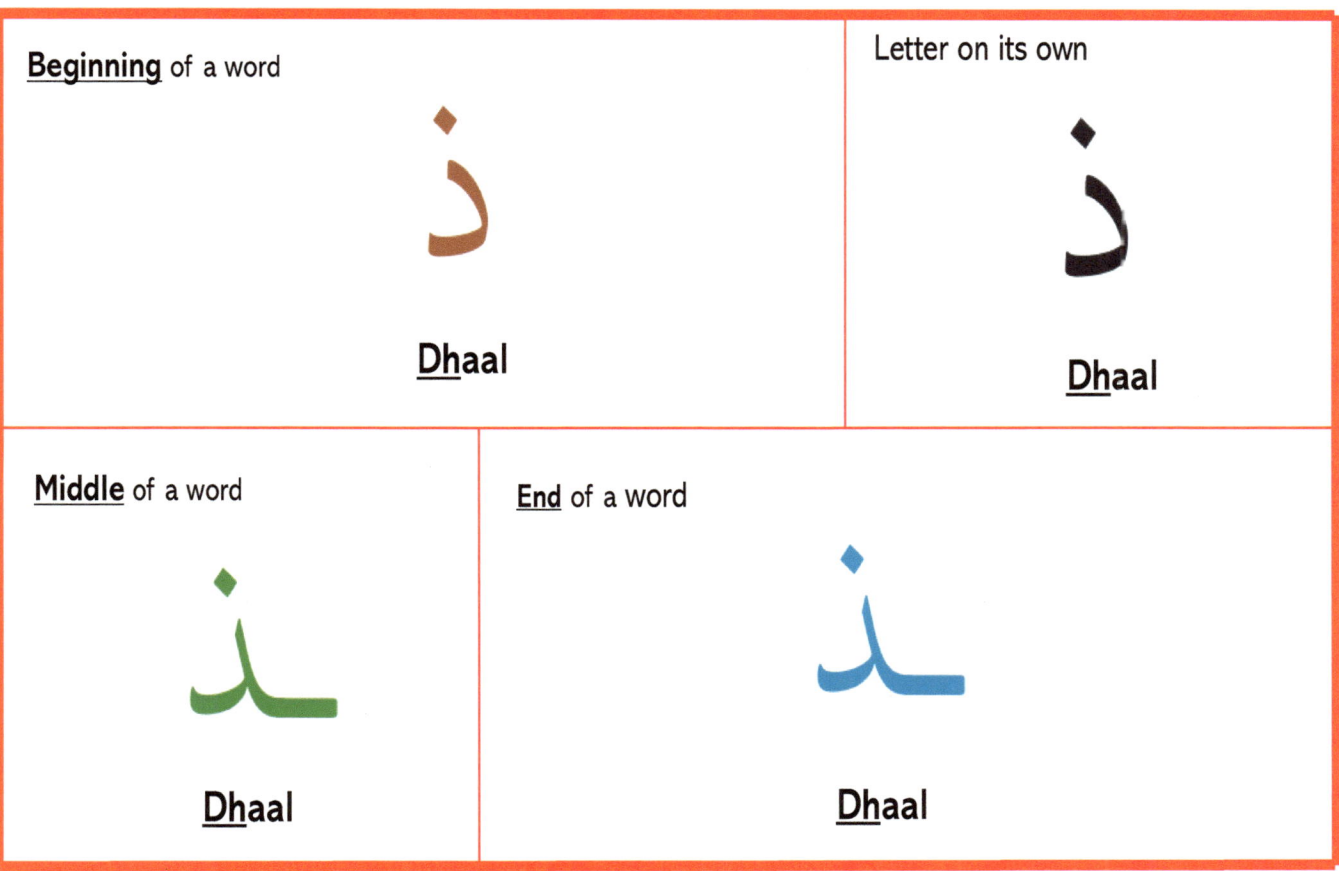

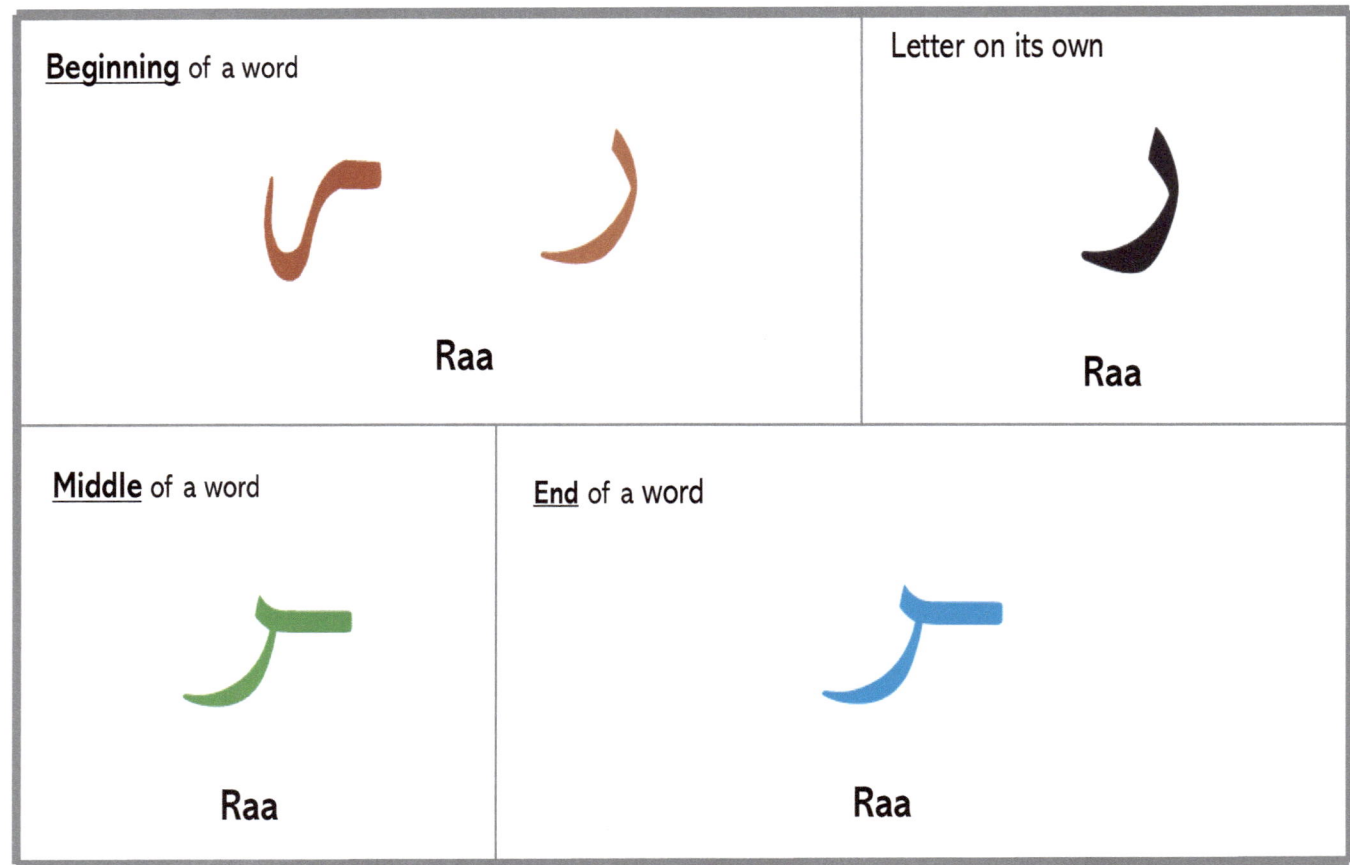

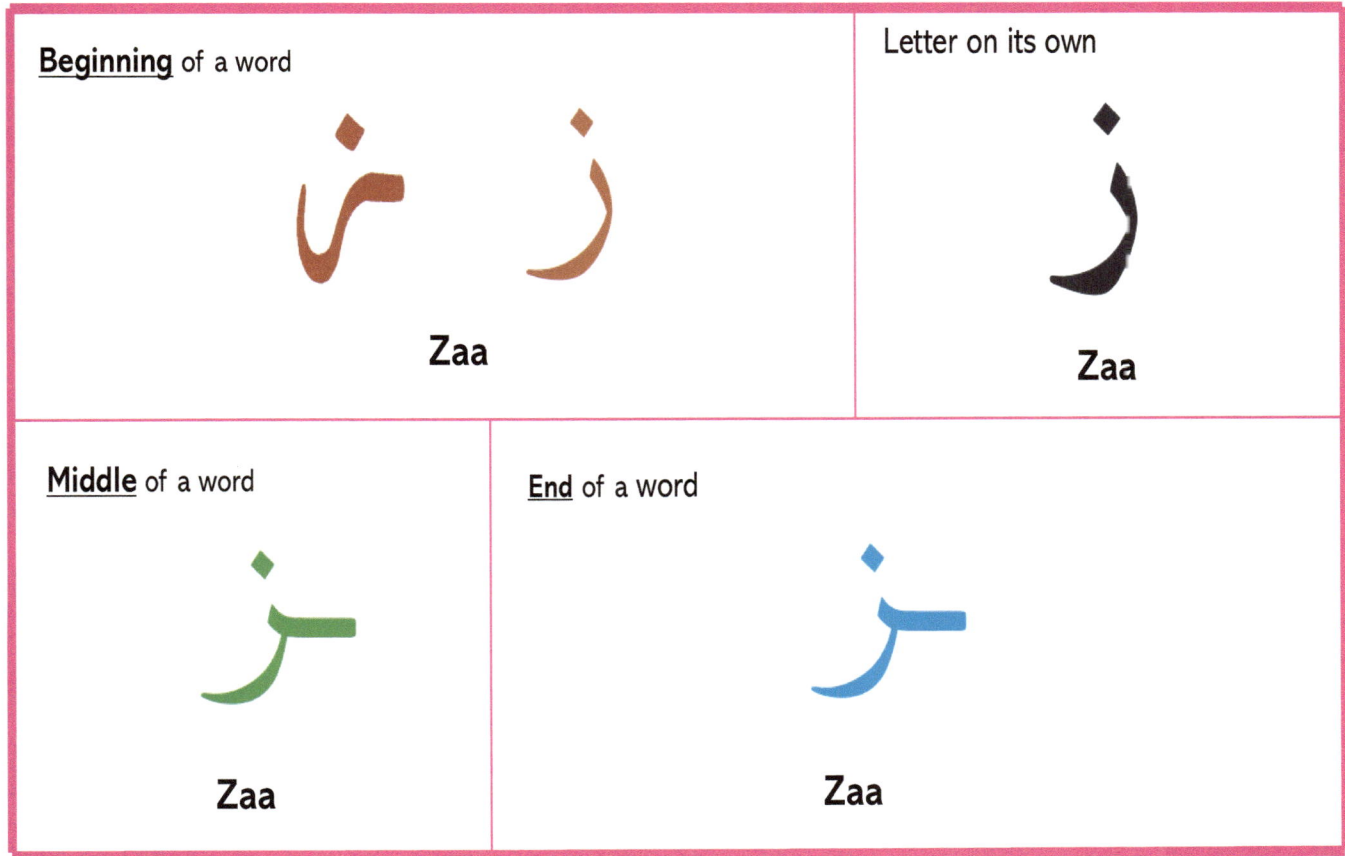

Beginning of a word سـ Seen	Letter on its own س Seen
Middle of a word ـسـ Seen	**End** of a word ـس Seen

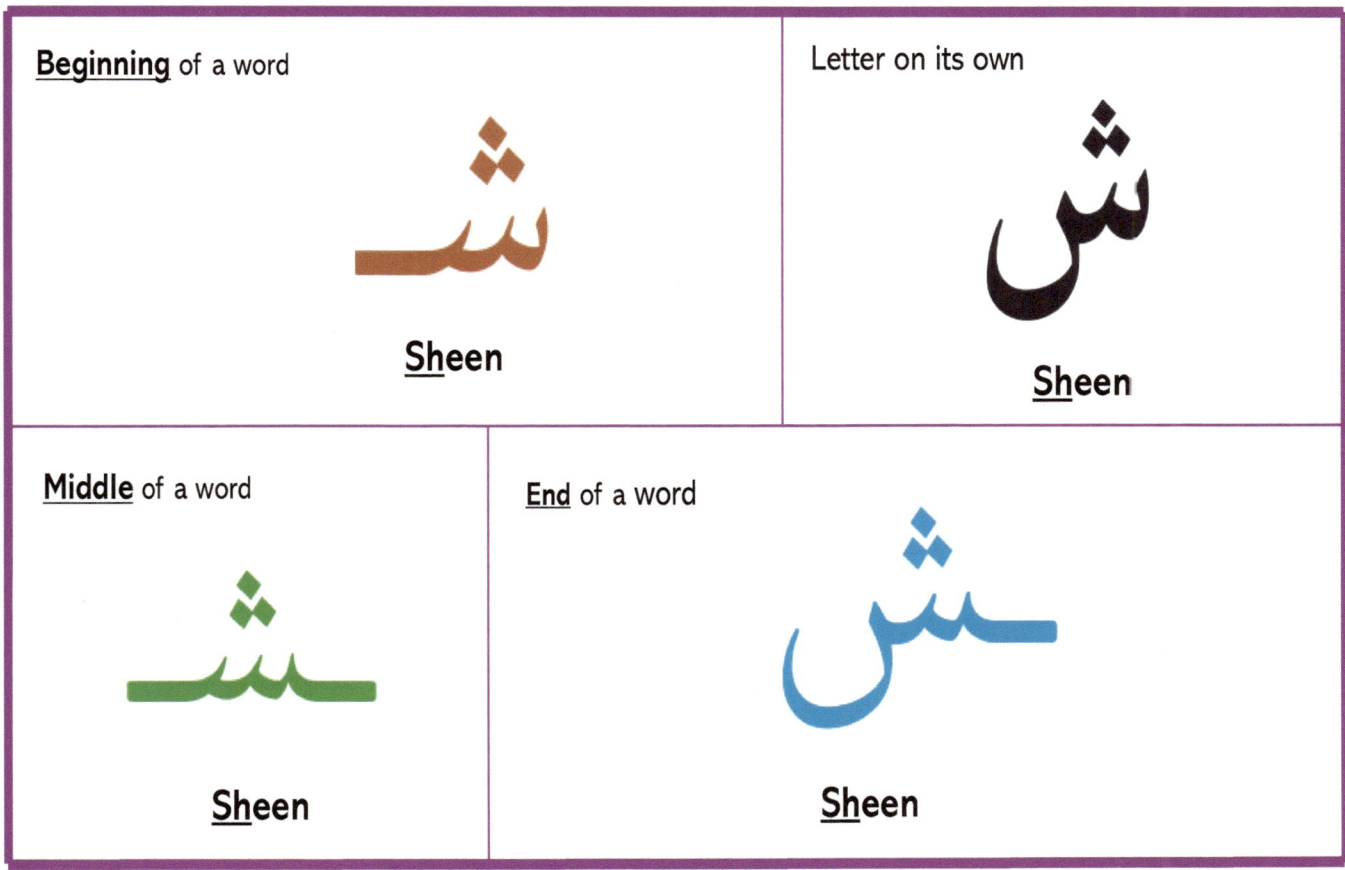

Beginning of a word صـ Saad	Letter on its own ص Saad
Middle of a word ـصـ Saad	**End** of a word ـص Saad

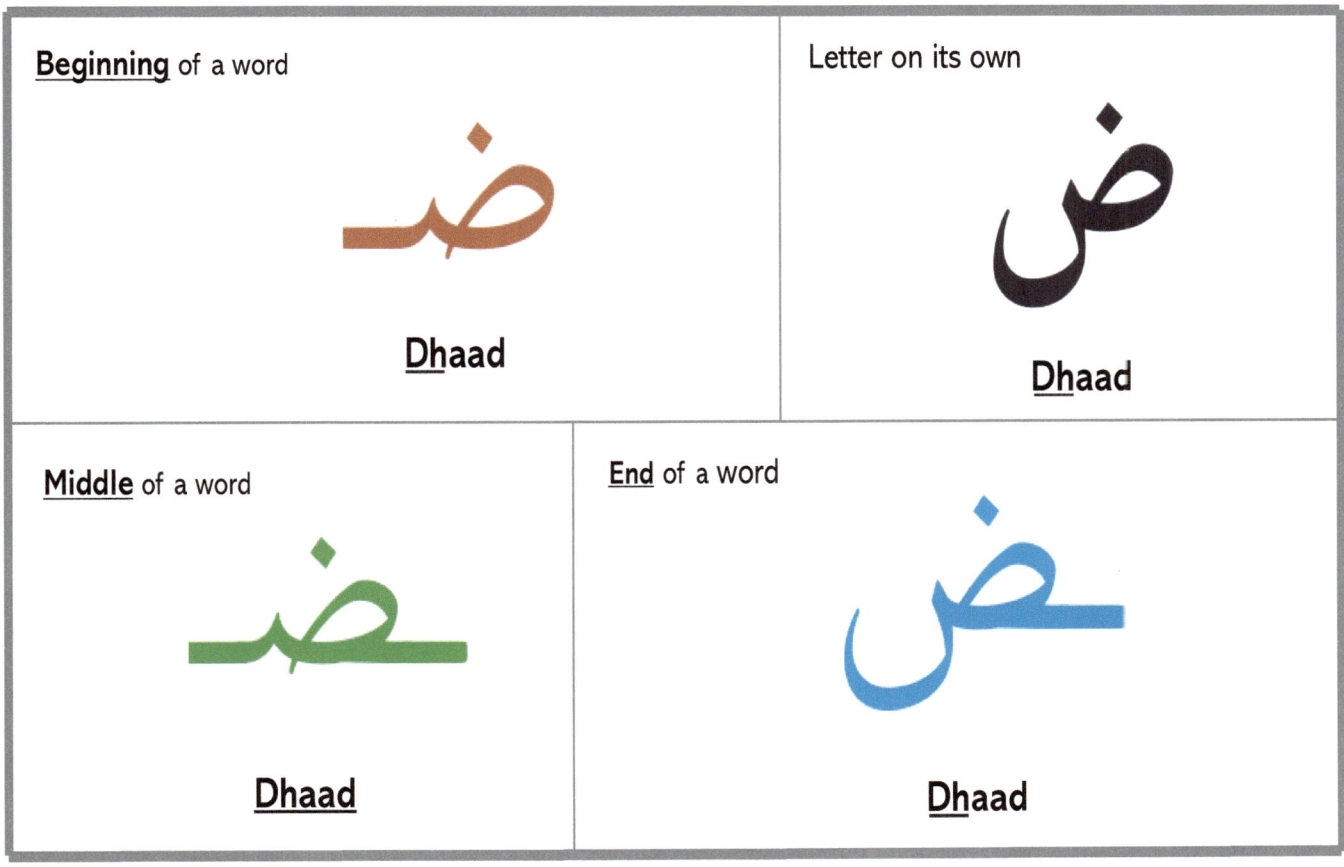

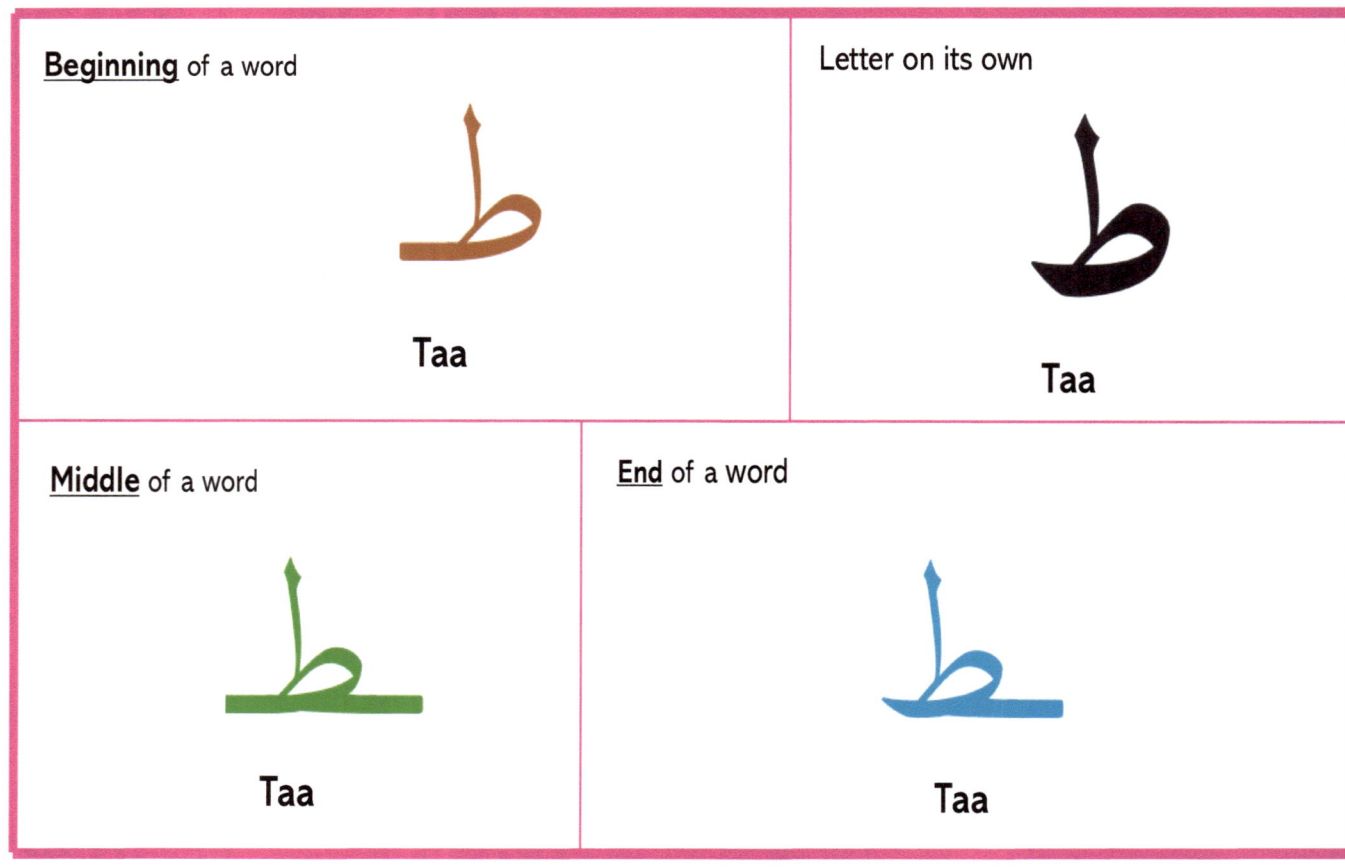

Beginning of a word ظ **Dhaa**	Letter on its own ظ **Dhaa**
Middle of a word ظ **Dhaa**	**End** of a word ظ **Dhaa**

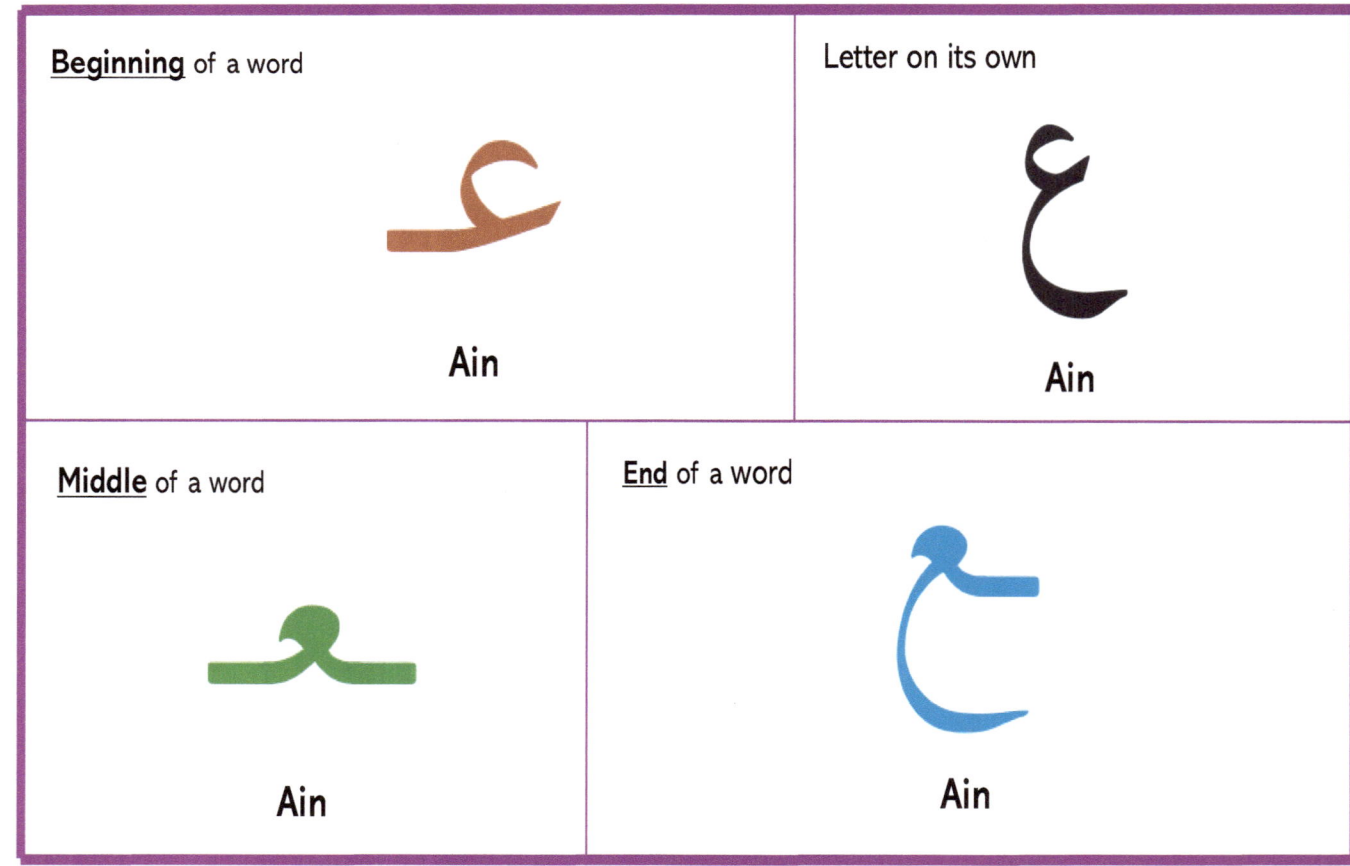

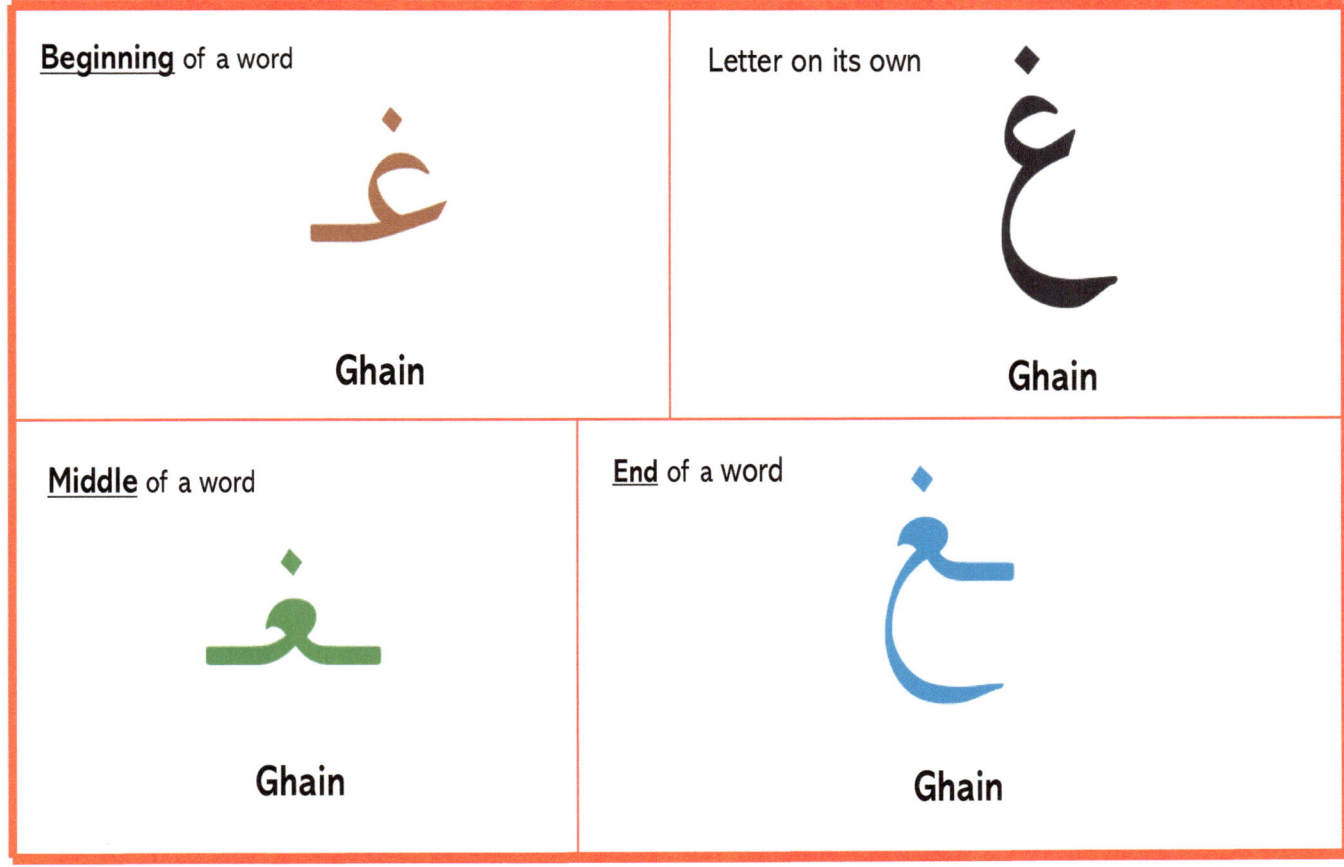

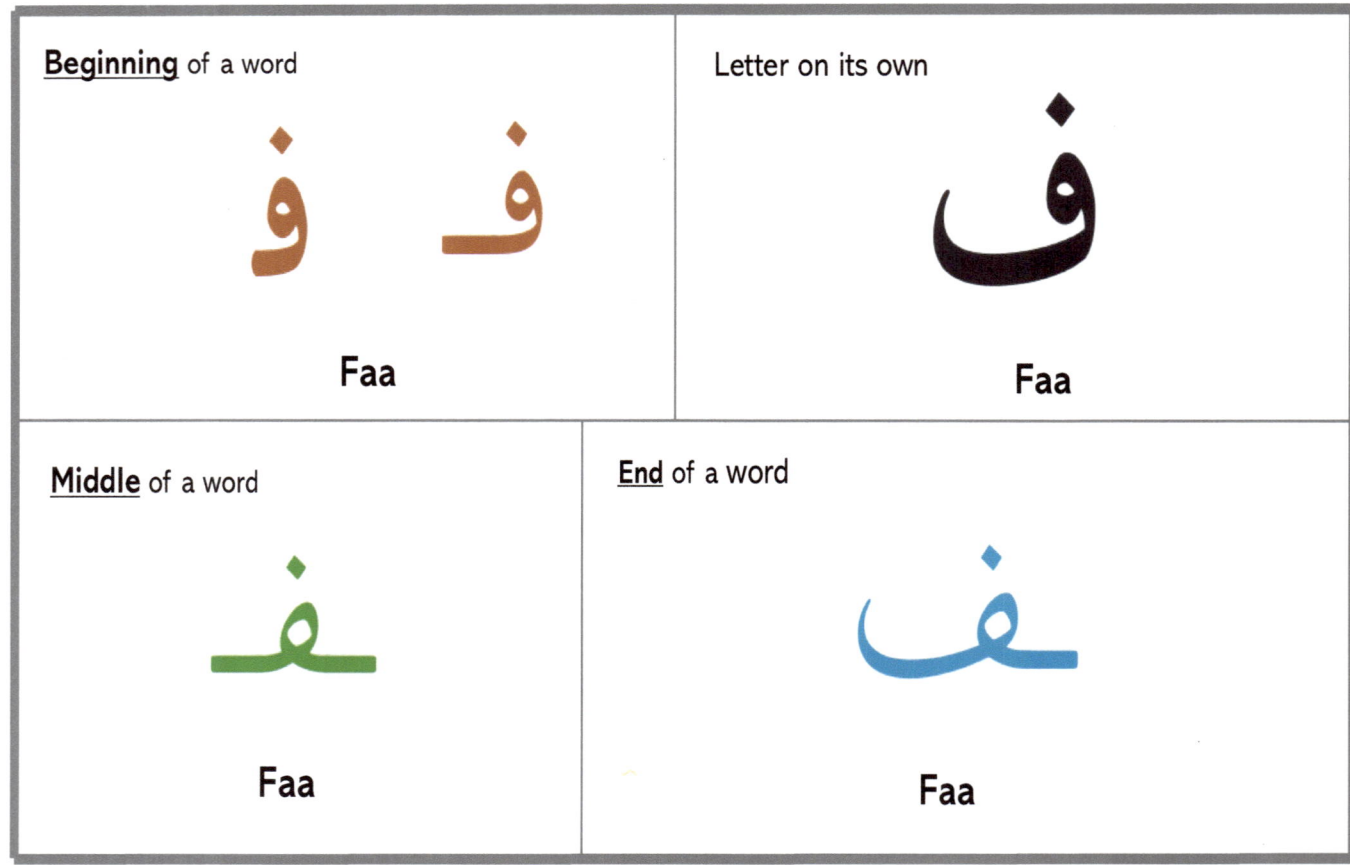

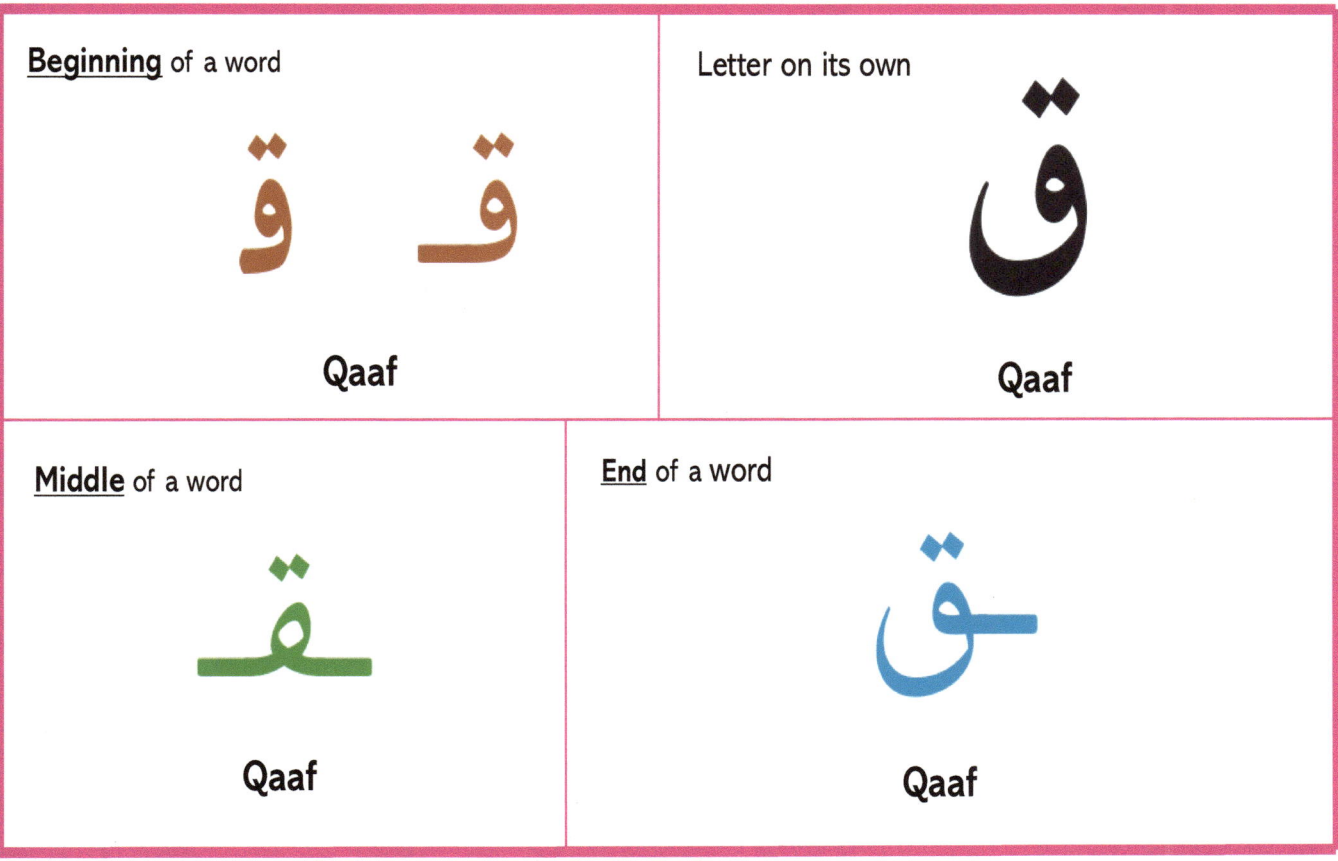

Beginning of a word ك ك **Kaaf**	Letter on its own ك **Kaaf**
Middle of a word ك **Kaaf**	**End** of a word ك **Kaaf**

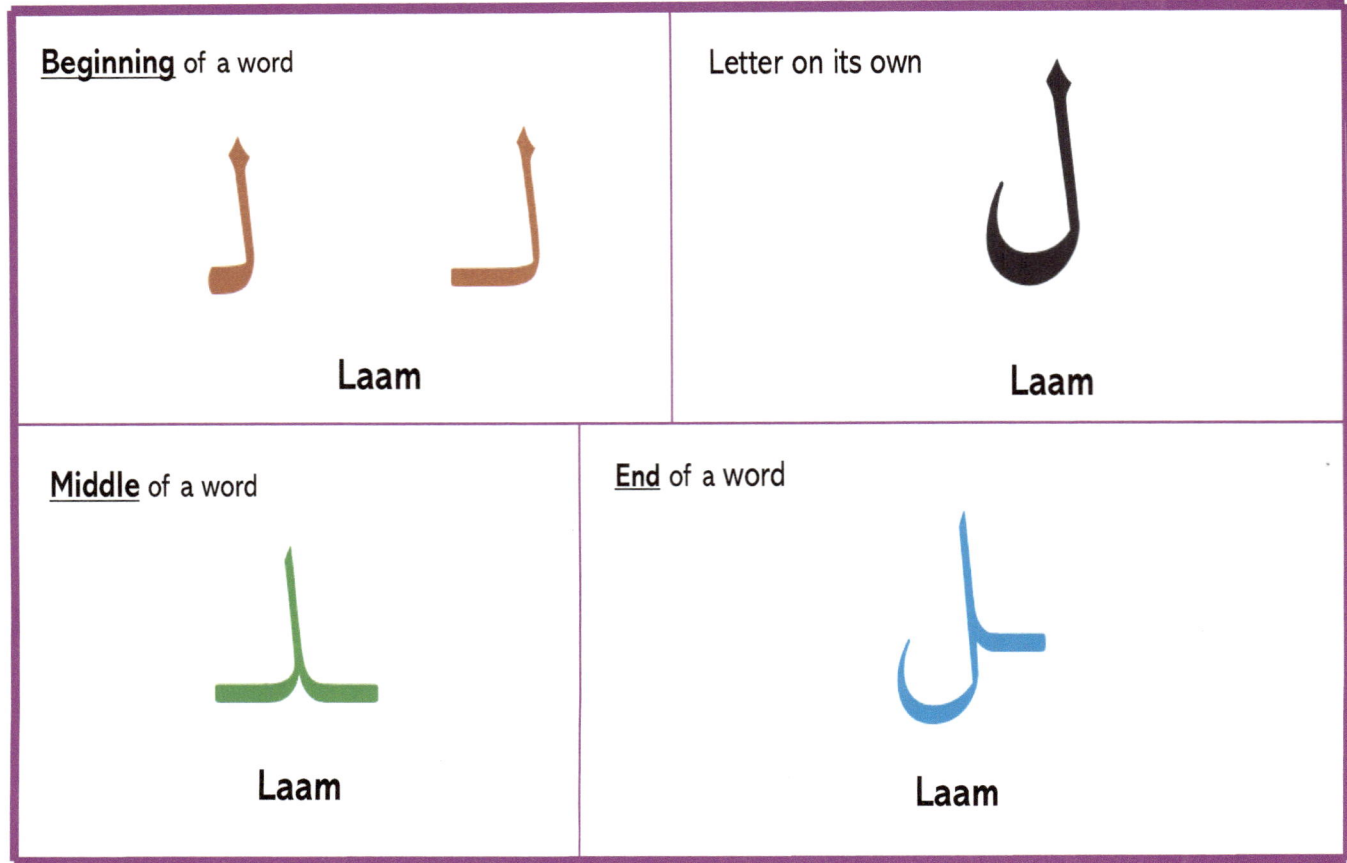

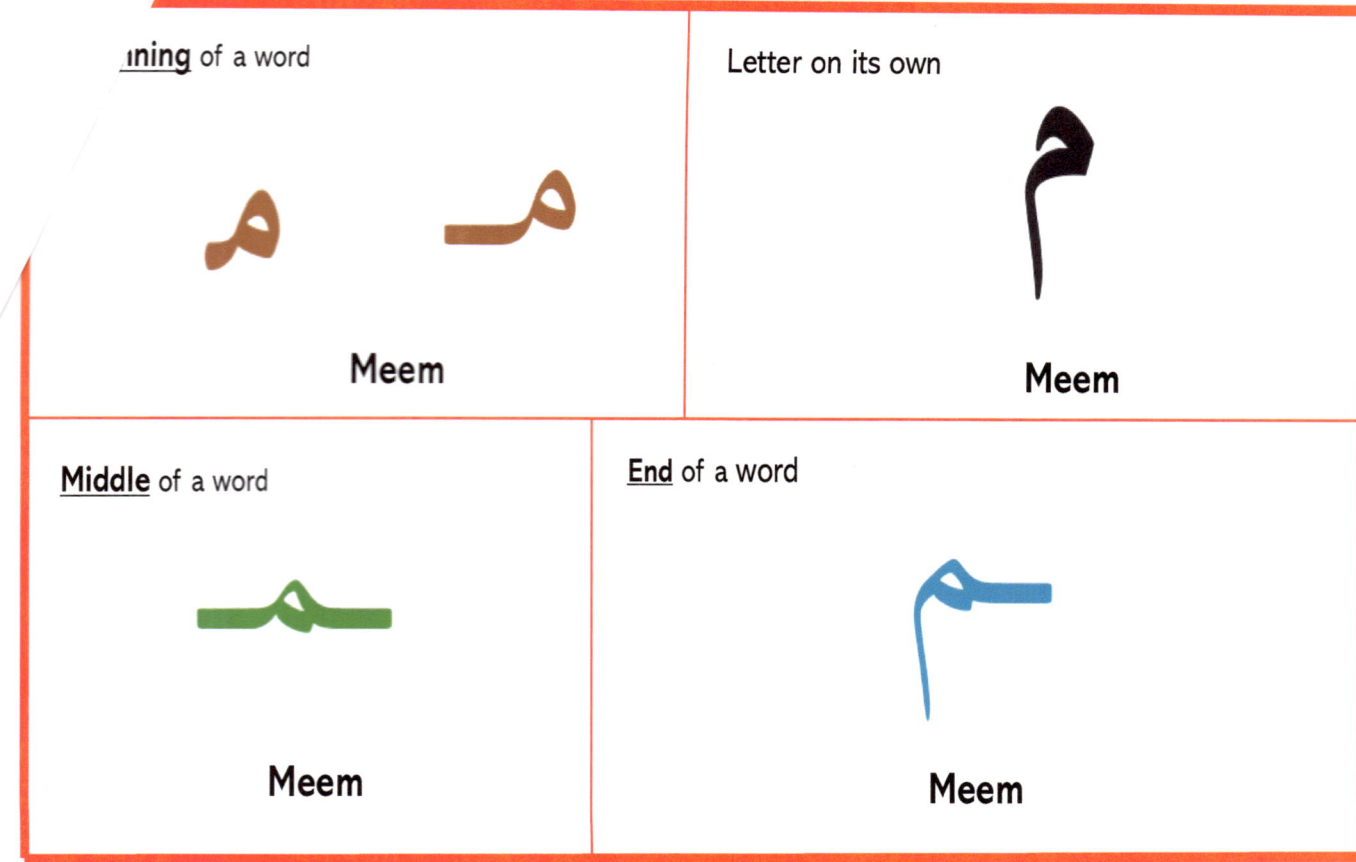

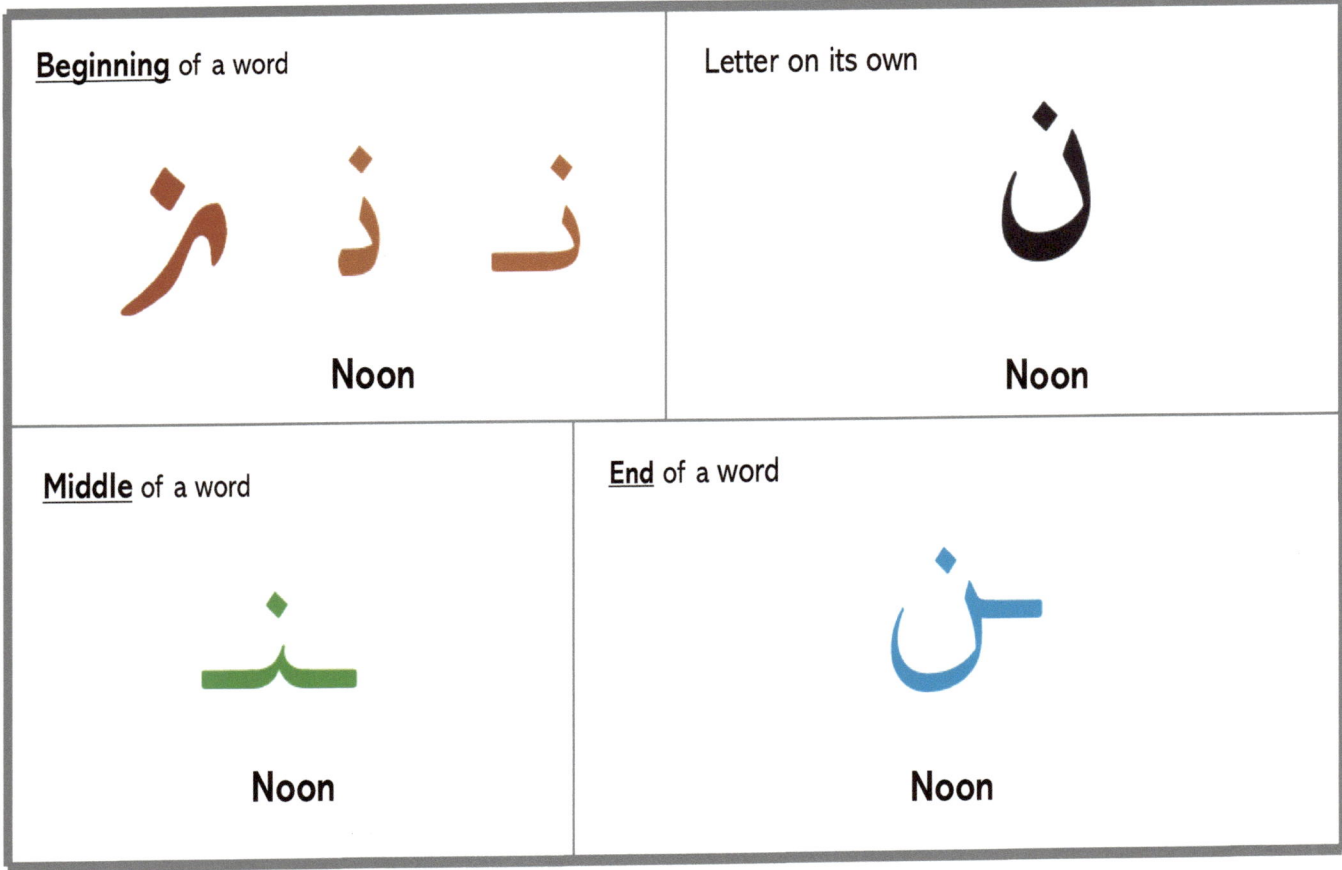

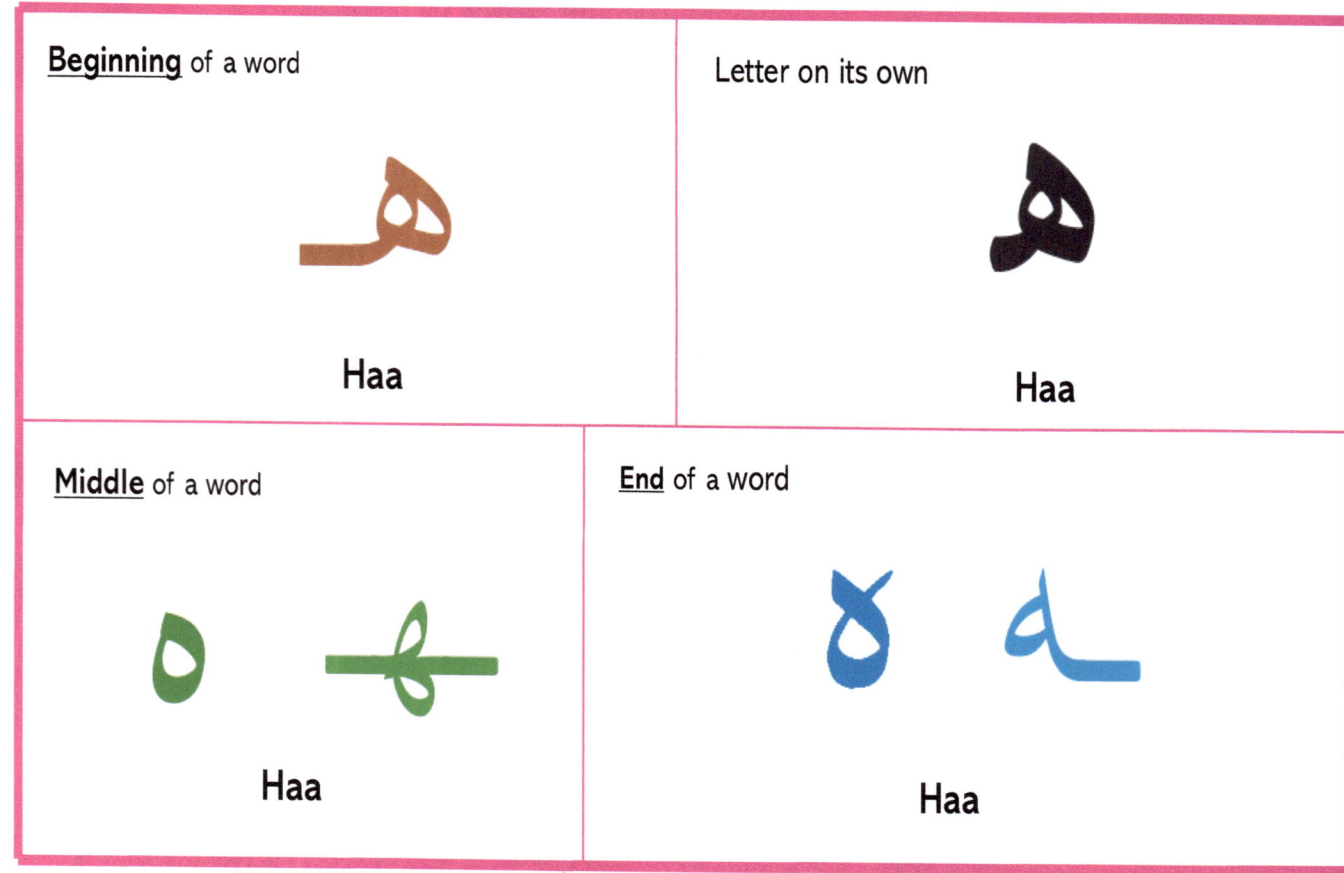

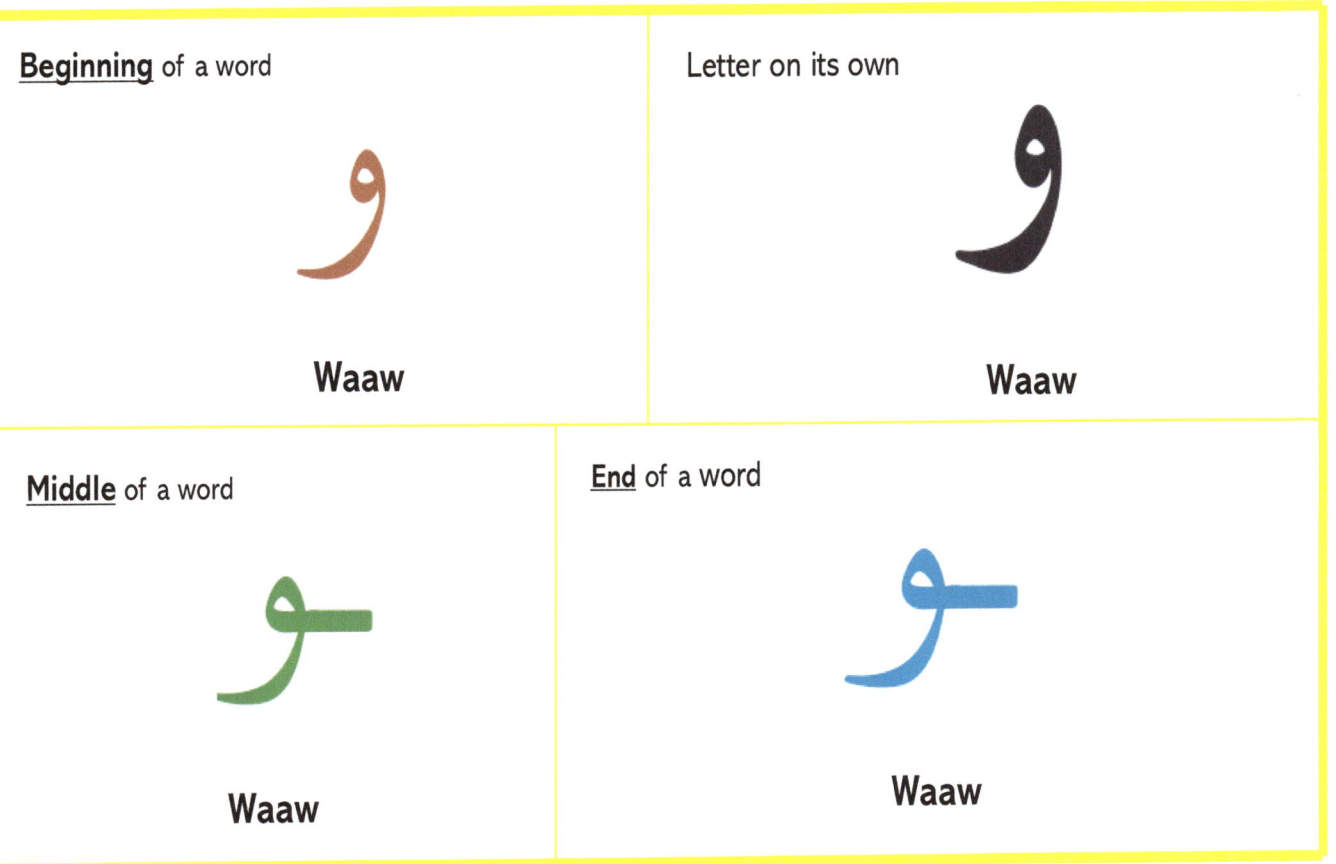

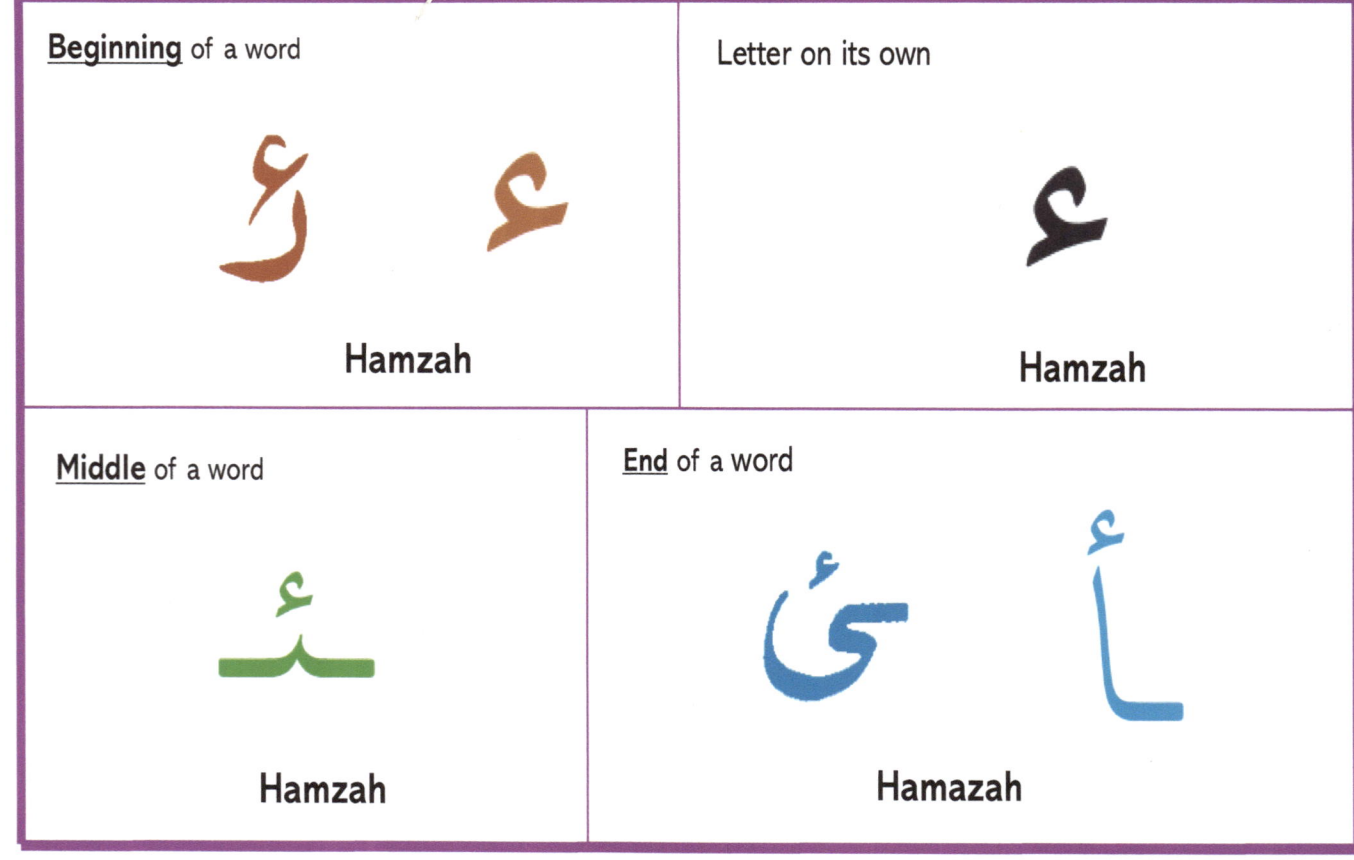

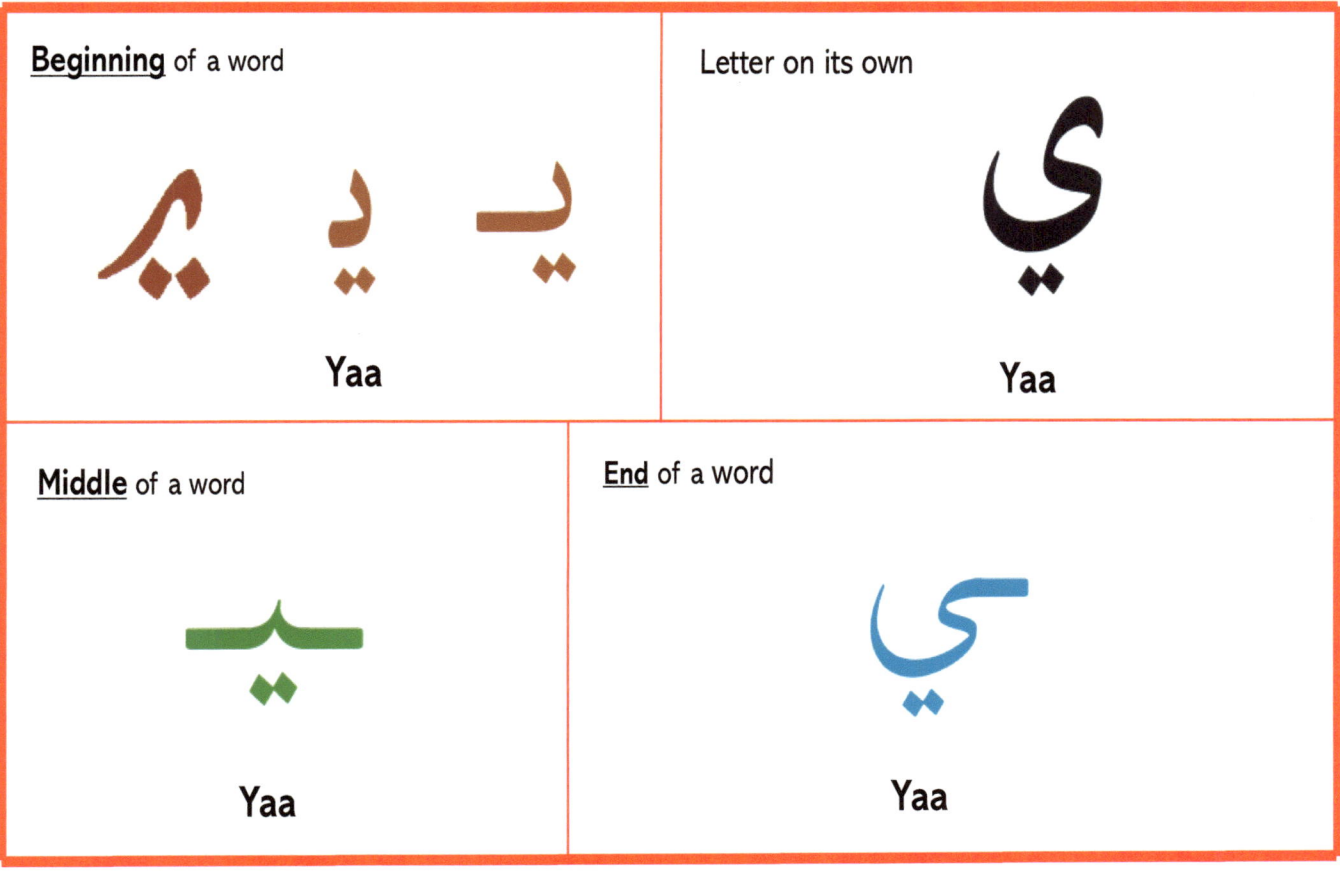

MY FIRST ARABIC LETTERS

This book is designed to support neurodiverse learners to recognise the Arabic alphabet letters with limited focus and attention. By using strategies such as colourful symantics and condensing the learning into a simple, one page visual for each letters.

It is an educational resource for teachers, Islamic schools and parents who are home schooling their child or any children who are at the beginners stage of their journey of learning to read the Qaidah.

RIZIA BEGUM

https://inspiredsendlearning.com/

www.ingramcontent.com/pod-product-compliance
Lightning Source LLC
Chambersburg PA
CBHW041118070526
44584CB00002B/210